Landforms

What is a Landform?

Rebecca Rissman

www.heinemannlibrary.co.uk
Visit our website to find out more information about Heinemann Library books.

To order:
☎ Phone +44 (0) 1865 888066
🖨 Fax +44 (0) 1865 314091
🖳 Visit www.heinemannlibrary.co.uk

Heinemann Library is an imprint of Capstone Global Library Limited, a company incorporated in England and Wales having its registered office at 7 Pilgrim Street, London, EC4V 6LB – Registered company number: 6695582

"Heinemann" is a registered trademark of Pearson Education Limited, under licence to Capstone Global Library Limited

Text © Capstone Global Library Limited 2009
First published in hardback in 2009

Edited by Rebecca Rissman, Siân Smith, and Charlotte Guillain
Designed by Kimberly Miracle and Joanna Malivoire
Picture research by Tracy Cummins
Originated by Capstone Global Library
Printed and bound in China by Leo Paper Products Ltd

ISBN 978 0 431 19425 7 (hardback)
13 12 11 10 09
10 9 8 7 6 5 4 3 2 1

British Library Cataloguing in Publication Data
Rissman, Rebecca.
  What is a landform?. -- (Acorn plus)
  1. Landforms--Juvenile literature.
  I. Title II. Series
  551.4'1-dc22

Acknowledgements
The author and publishers are grateful to the following for permission to reproduce copyright material: Age Fotostock p.**10** (© Gonzalo Azumendi); Alamy p.**16** (© Leslie Garland Picture Library); Corbis pp.**9 right** (© Jonathan Blair), **14** (©Pablo Corral Vega); Getty Images pp.**5** (© The Image Bank/Steve Allen), **6** (© National Geographic/Michael Melford), **7** (© Science Faction/ Ed Darack), **8** (© Haas), **11 left** (© Look/Hermann Erber), **13 right** (© National Geographic/Thomas J. Abercrombie), **17 middle** (© Altrendo Travel), **17 right** (© The Image Bank/Michael Blann), **19 left** (© Tom Till), **20 right** (© Paul Chesley), **21 left** (© Philippe Bourseiller); NASA Goddard Space Flight Center p.**4** (Visual Earth); Photolibrary pp.**9 left** (© Photodisc/Amanda Clement), **11 right** (© Photographer's Choice/Peter Pinnock), **12** (© Oxford Scientific/ David Clapp); Shuterstock pp.**4 insert** (© Andrea Danti), **13 left** (© Jeanne Hatch), **15** (© juliengrondin), **17 left** (© L. F. File), **18 left** (© Alexey Stiop), **18 right** (© Galyna Andrushko), **19 right** (© iamanewbee), **20 left** (© Jason McCartney).

Front cover photograph reproduced with permission of Getty Images (© Philippe Bourseiller). Back cover photograph reproduced with permission of Shutterstock (© iamanewbee).

We would like to thank Nancy Harris and Adriana Scalise for their help in the preparation of this book.

Every effort has been made to contact copyright holders of any material reproduced in this book. Any omissions will be rectified in subsequent printings if notice is given to the publisher.

Contents

Some words are shown in bold, **like this**. They are explained in "Words to know" on page 23.

What are landforms?

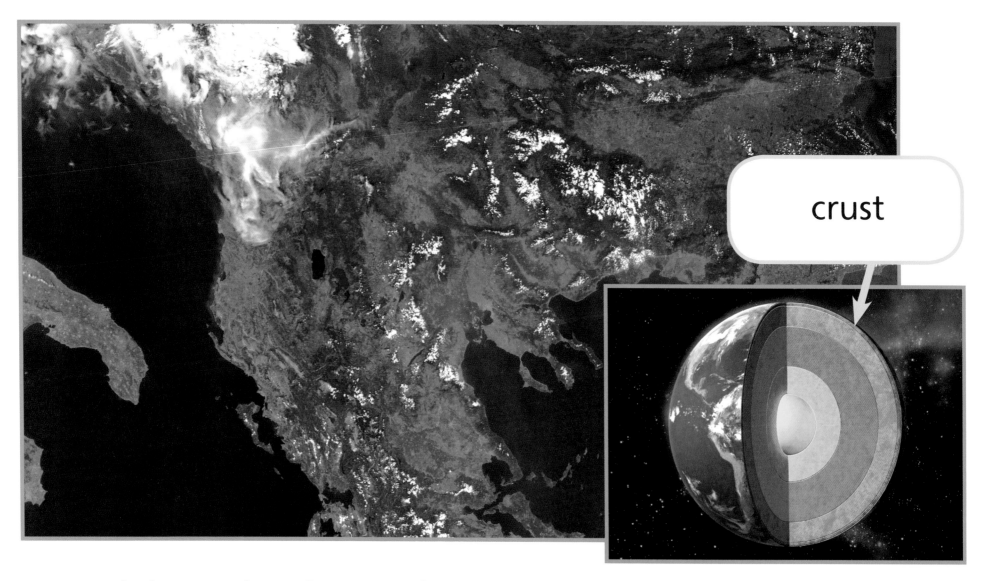

crust

Earth is made of many **layers**. The top layer of Earth is called its **crust**. Earth's crust can be many different shapes.

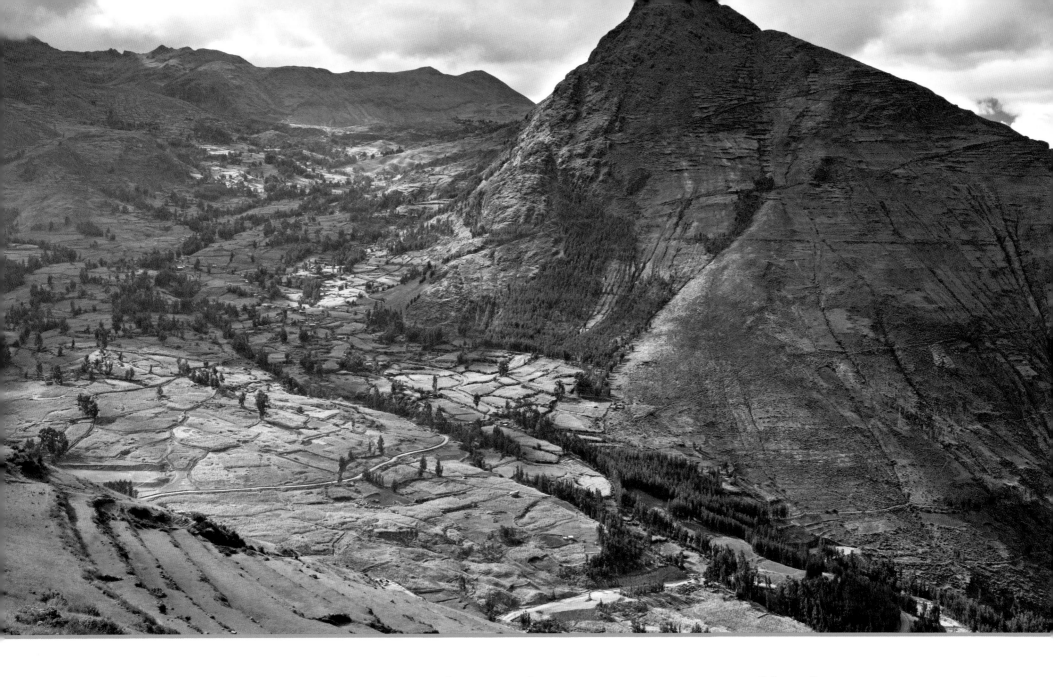

The different shapes of Earth's crust are called landforms. There are different types of landforms.

Earth's **crust** is not living. But Earth's crust is always changing.

When Earth's crust moves, new landforms are made.
Landforms show us how Earth's crust can change.

Islands

An island is a landform. An island is land that is **surrounded** by water.

Islands can be far apart. Islands can be close together. A group of islands is called a **chain**.

Caves

A cave is a landform. A cave is an opening in the Earth's surface.

Caves can be found in mountains. Caves can be found underwater.

Mountains

A mountain is a landform. A mountain is land that rises high above the ground. All mountains are made of rock.

Some mountains stand alone. Some mountains are close together. A group of mountains is called a **range**.

Volcanoes

A volcano is a landform. A volcano is a mountain with a hole at the top. Hot, liquid rock called **lava** can come out of this hole.

lava

Some volcanoes **erupt**. Lava comes out of the hole at the top of the volcano. Lava can flow down the sides of the volcano.

Valleys

A valley is a landform. A valley is a low area of land between mountains or hills.

glacier

Some valleys have streams at the bottom. Some valleys have rivers at the bottom. Some valleys have **glaciers** at the bottom!

What is different?

island

mountain

How is this island different from this mountain?

cave

valley

How is this cave different from this valley?

Answers on page 22.

What is similar?

mountain

island

How is this mountain like this island?

volcano

valley

How is this volcano like this valley?

Answers on page 22.

Answers

What is different?

The island is different from the mountain because it is **surrounded** by water. There is sand on the island but there is snow on the mountain.

The shape of the cave is different to the shape of the valley. The cave is a hole in rock. The valley is a low area of land with high sides. Only the valley is covered in trees.

What is similar?

The mountain is like the island because they are both made out of rock and are both covered with trees.

The volcano is like the valley because they are both made out of rock. The sides of the valley are grey and the outside of the volcano is grey.

Words to know

chain	group of islands
compare	look at two or more things to see how they are the same and how they are different
crust	the top layer of the Earth's surface
erupt	burst out
glacier	huge amount of ice which moves slowly
lava	very hot rock that has turned into liquid
layer	made up of different parts that lie on top of each other
range	group of mountains
surrounded	has something all the way around it

Index

Notes for parents and teachers

Before reading

Tell the children that Earth is made of many layers. The top layer is called the crust. The crust makes different shapes, which are called landforms. Explain that one type of landform is a mountain. Ask children if they know of a different type of landform? Tell children that other landforms are islands, caves, volcanoes, and valleys. Together, create a chart entitled "Landforms." Write the following titles to create three columns: "What You Know," "What You Want to Know," and "What You've Learned." Discuss and fill in the first two columns with the children.

After reading

• Continue discussing and filling in the chart with the children. Ask children what they learned from this book and fill in the third column together.

• Encourage children to discuss the similarities and differences between the landforms. After the discussion give each child a piece of paper. Ask them to draw a picture of two landforms that are similar on one side of the paper, and to draw two landforms that are different on the other.